IMAGES OF
WALES

IMAGES OF
WALES

FROM A DECADE OF CHANGE
·THE 1970s·

RICHARD GAUNT

FONTHILL

Fonthill Media Limited
Fonthill Media LLC
www.fonthillmedia.com
office@fonthillmedia.com

First published in the United Kingdom 2014

British Library Cataloguing in Publication Data:
A catalogue record for this book is available from the British Library

ISBN 978-1-78155-243-8

Typeset in Minion Pro 11/14
Printed and bound in England

Contents

one
Introduction

For those of us who can think back to Wales in the 1970s much seems familiar enough; the same mountains and rivers, lots of history, plenty of development along the southern and northern coasts and mainly grass and sheep in between. Much of the infrastructure has not changed either, as anyone trying to get from North Wales to South Wales in a hurry knows all too well.

In many other ways, though, that era now seems almost unrecognisably distant. These were the days before S4C (opened in 1982) and devolution—indeed the proposals considered in the 1979 referendum were defeated. At a UK level, without trying to encroach on the job of historians it is worth recalling that the 1970s saw the 3-day week, when widespread industrial action led to the UK government restricting the use of electricity to conserve coal stocks at the power stations. The 1978–79 'Winter of Discontent' saw even wider industrial action. There was the IMF bailout, inflation hitting well over 20 per cent, and a series of attempts to resolve it all politically through consensus and rational argument. That wheel turned: Mrs Thatcher was to become Prime Minister in 1979 with a rather different agenda.

Serious stuff—but it was also true that the top 10 singles for 1974 included non-classics like 'Tiger Feet' (Mud) and 'Sugar Baby Love' (The Rubettes). The less said about fashion statements like 'disco' flared trousers and careless use of glitter and Spandex the better.

The Welsh economy—then as now—attracted much comment and concern, but the sheer scale of some of the enforced changes Wales has had to face demand recognition.

One has to be careful about stereotypes: in fact, more people play soccer than rugby in Wales, and I know more who cannot sing than can. But the changes to the coal and steel industries are real enough. In 1970 the NCB had over 60,000 miners in South Wales alone. In steel, if we could go back to 1970 names like Shotton, Brymbo, Ebbw Vale, Velindre, DuPort and East Moors would mean 'steelworks' not 'redevelopment opportunity.'

Left Beautiful mountains, rivers, coastlines: (relatively) unchanging and (fairly) unspoilt.

Below Lots and lots of history.

A land of mines and steelworks.

Above And terrace housing, often in hilly surroundings which might have promoted physical fitness … but mostly didn't.

Below It was not just coal and steel. Manufacturing generally was going through a torrid time. This is the site of the former Powell Duffryn works in Cardiff (not finally closed until the 1990s, but with major layoffs during previous decades). Like the smile of the Cheshire cat, the boss's car space lives on after offices and erecting shops are long gone.

And yet it did not necessarily feel too bad: GDP figures for the UK grew steadily over the decade and property prices rose appreciably, so a lot of people started to *feel* better off just from owning a house—on paper they had significant wealth, maybe for the first time, although getting at it might not be easy. Figures for Wales lagged behind UK averages, but at least there were enough encouraging signs to see some redevelopment of town centres (St David's Centre in Cardiff opened in 1981), and investment in retail parks. Some new jobs turned up in the 1970s but—as in later decades—not really enough, and quite a few lacked sufficiently deep roots for the long-term.

Wales has long-established religious traditions: 20,000 saints buried on Bardsey, the missionary work of St David, the religious revivals of the nineteenth and early twentieth centuries, that sort of thing. Churches and chapels were still numerous and influential—but decreasingly so as the decades rolled on.

So that is part of the context for what follows. This is a book of photographs I took in the 1970s (a few are later, where they seemed relevant) which pick up some of the everyday details which caught my eye as these changes swirled around.

How did these photographs come to be taken? The easiest explanation I can give is that I had already developed an interest—maybe a habit is a better way of putting it—for taking images of day-to-day life in industrial areas . It started when I lived in the North of England. There too were coal mines and steelworks and tough-looking towns which already looked as if they might not have much of a future. But they provided plenty of gritty opportunities for anyone with a camera, particularly one who had borrowed maybe too many books on 'pictorial' photography from the local library.

When I moved to Wales I was mindful that demolition or redevelopment was on its way to various places near where I lived and worked, and set out to picture some before it was too late. By the end of the 1970s I had accumulated several thousand black and white negatives and colour slides on these themes.

It might all have become landfill, but Alan Sutton and his colleagues had published some of my steam engine material from the North East, and we started to discuss more general sights you could once see every day—but often can't see at all now.

Inevitably the images give a partial view at best, and are highly personal. There is probably a bias towards the darker, less 'pretty' aspects of those places I did photograph and there are occasional slips into pretentiousness, for which I apologise. I also tended to get excited by snow or fog, so the images are not necessarily flattering.

Biggest regret? So little material of Wrexham, Swansea, and their surrounding areas. I have spent a lot of time there and enjoyed my visits, but have few photographs for various reasons. So if there no images of your favourite bit of Wales, or it's all too dark and grim, I'm sorry.

Quite a few employers were enticed into Wales, but did not stay. Here are two who did: Bisley make office furniture in Newport; Radiochemicals came to Forest Farm, north of Cardiff. They were quickly renamed Amersham—although this did not seem to make much difference to local concerns about radioactivity, whether based on hard evidence or some of the other stuff. Various changes of ownership and technology have taken place, and a partial relocation to Pencoed, but this remains an example of good quality, science-based employment succeeding in globally competitive markets: pity there aren't a few more…

Witness next to the steelworks: Christ Church in Ebbw Vale.

All sorts of interesting details. Doorways on property soon to be redeveloped; the celebrity endorsement of Lyons Maid? David Nixon, TV magician in the days of black and white screens. Primitive Place is in Beaufort, its name linking with the Primitive Methodists rather than making any sort of comment about the locality. A big era too for graffiti—and mainly mindless 'tagging' not anything witty or original. Difficult to ignore, though, contributing to an unloved, unlovely appearance in many public places.

Scrapyards brought plenty of photographic interest, whether dealing with limousines or worn out Valley buses. Public attitudes and regulations were more relaxed in the 1970s than they are now, but even so it's difficult to believe that burning bus tyres was exactly good practice. The main priority, though, was getting the metal components off to the furnaces: apparently that didn't include the long-suffering Gardner diesel engines, normally destined for yet more hard labour powering Third World fishing boats, or so I was told at the time.

Left and below I had a go at capturing the very mundane aspects of life, but it wasn't easy and there could be hints of pretentiousness. Take picturing Welsh rain, for example—here with an Austin A40. It certainly captures aspects of life for me in Wales in the 1970s, but probably says more about not having much to do on a wet Sunday afternoon. And like the image of the net curtains and terraced housing, you could probably take a similar photograph tomorrow—provided you would be prepared to compromise on the no longer plentiful A40, I suppose.

Opposite A lot of terraced housing remains, usually benefiting from repeated grant-aided refurbishment work, once the value of established communities worked its way past some fairly determined moves in favour of 'slum clearance'. The streets here, in Cardiff's docks area went before this change in attitudes had won through.

Technically, I arrived with a much-loved brute of an Exakta Varex IIb camera, funded by work on a construction site back in 1966. This had seen a lot of film and much adventure by the early 1970s, when it got replaced by Canon kit. Canon AE1s are much better cameras than Exaktas, but I cannot say the pictures were any better: I suspect that operating without much in the way of built-in metering, leave alone more modern mysteries like autofocus, makes you think about what you're trying to achieve a bit more.

The biggest constraint of all, though, was other calls on my time. I have been to most places in Wales over the years—mostly many times over—but sneaking off to take some photographs of back streets or a particularly well-lit spoil heap might be difficult if I was supposed to be working, or had small children in tow.

I am mainly a photographer of places, but including people can improve a drab image no end, giving scale and interest. People would often come up and have a chat—typically lads who simply wanted to see what I was doing—and sometimes they got pictured too. There was not much consistency here, though, and there are many people in Wales I wish I had photographed over the years, but sadly did not.

When I moved to Wales in 1969 I had a couple of things on my mind. Growing up in the North of England, I really had no knowledge of Wales or the Welsh at all. Apparently a great-uncle had moved to Colwyn Bay many years before and started a business, with mixed results—but then died before I was born, and in any case the links between Colwyn Bay and Cardiff seemed a bit tenuous then (and maybe are not a lot stronger now).

'What's worth taking a picture of round here?' Lads want to see what's going on.

On first appearances, a young lady of a particular kind. On looking closer, a shop window dummy who's seen better days.

Then I also had to think about the implications of full-time employment: I won't say 'career' for I had signed up to work for British Steel on the not-very- substantial reasoning that they had offered me £50 per year more than anyone else, and I didn't fancy living in the Home Counties much.

Most pressing of all, though, was whether I was properly free from what various humorists refer to as Montezuma's revenge. I had spent the month before arriving in Cardiff in Mexico, funded by a couple of months work in Charlotte NC, and was my usual healthy self—right until it was time to leave. Then my gastric system became the battleground many other travellers will recognise. A pharmacist in New York City who guaranteed a cure was overstating his powers by some distance, as I found out during the induction course for my new job, when I urgently had to leave a senior figure's presentation (whether visionary or motivational I cannot now remember) and get closer to some porcelain down the corridor. 'Fair comment—he has that effect on a lot of people' was one response from a more experienced staff member. In truth, though, BSC was in all kinds of trouble, and poorly equipped indeed to face the turbulent 1970s. Less than two years later I was gone. And if I had joined British Airways, or Pilkingtons? Well, who knows? I don't suppose I'd be writing about everyday life in Wales many years later.

Looking ahead, job, domestic and social issues sorted themselves out (to some extent, anyway) and by the end of the 1970s British Steel was well behind me, I was married, with two children (and two more to come), a house by the park, and all of that. As for the photographic habit, it's never really gone away, though I tend to find fewer subjects that seem genuinely interesting. I suppose it's probably the aging process.

I think that's probably enough of a preamble, and it's time to look at particular aspects of Wales in the 1970s. In terms of a structure for what follows, this can never be a comprehensive, definitive view of Wales. It is personal, selective—biased even. Looking over what had caught my eye all those years ago, there seemed to be a mix of themes (the seaside, churches/chapels and so on) and locations (the Valleys, the West/North, and the rest). Rather than opt for just one of these groups of categories and squeezing everything into it, I've gone for a mix of both. Bear with me. Please.

two
Cardiff

Where to start? When you look at maps or satellite images it is clear that Wales is mainly rural; many parts have colourful and complex histories going back to the time when Stonehenge was being built from Pembrokeshire stone. Proud linguistic and cultural traditions are strongest in the west and north, not the populous but more cosmopolitan south-east.

But for me, it makes sense to retrace my footsteps in Wales only as far as the south of Cardiff, and specifically to Butetown and the Docks. That is where I was based for several months during my early days with BSC. This area, never in my experience known as Tiger Bay, has since been reinvented as Cardiff Bay, with countless wine bars and what I believe are sometimes known as eateries.

In 1970, though, that was all some way in the future. It was easier to identify the last glimmers of what had once been a system for delivering vast wealth through trading and managing coal and shipping. The world's first £1 million cheque was written in the Coal Exchange; there was just a hint of how it used to be as a small number of aging, well-dressed men slid into posh cars at lunchtime to pop home, get into town for a few minutes .... Or who knows what.

The Pier Head was not what it had once been, either. *Waverley* still called in season, but the much-loved P. & A. Campbell Bristol Channel paddle steamers were gone. Mainly the basis for countless days out to Weston and the rest of the Bristol Channel, they had once been important as basic transportation. When I started playing ruby, some of the older selection cards were still around which included 'report at the pier head' as an option if the club had an away fixture in the South West of England. These kinds of arrangements could not really survive in the era of the Severn Bridge, increasingly available road transport, and cheap foreign holidays. Nice to see *Waverley* and *Balmoral* still in action, but with the barrage in place, the closest they get to Cardiff is Penarth.

A lot of the housing in the Docks and the rest of central Cardiff looked clapped out, with no real future. Maybe that was a premature judgement: the best of what remained has become sought-after and, in some parts distinctly fashionable.

The Cardiff skyline in 1970 (from Roath). Essentially low-rise and domestic, with the steelworks to the left.

It would, of course, be quite wrong to portray Cardiff in the 1970s as grey and grimy throughout. There were a lot more leafy suburbs than slums, all those aloof-looking public buildings in Cathays Park and lots of fine parkland. Indeed, most people I knew spent all their time in this sort of environment and could forget all about the gritty bits. As a reminder of this side of town, an important-looking man is striding past playing children in Bute Park and the cherry blossom which appears in the middle of Cathays Park every year—both within easy walking distance of all those newly-opening shops in the first phase of the St David's Centre. (I suspect that the Cathays Park image dates from the early 1980s: the vast extension to what was then the Welsh Office didn't open until late 1979. It seems I was also playing about with a yellow filter to make the sky more dramatic).

Offices in The Docks: once a machine for generating large sums of money for a wealthy few—and a reasonable living for many more. But the peak year was 1913, and by 1970 the goose that laid the the golden eggs was either dead or had received a better offer from somewhere else.

A few of the firms in Mountstuart Square—once the epicentre of all of that trading and broking and financing—were hanging on, the echoes of the good times still just about lingering. More and more buildings were becoming derelict, though, with local lads exploring past grandeur.

The redevelopment of Cardiff Bay which has taken place in the years since this bleak low point has, apparently, been a major commercial success. By no means every empty building has been refurbished, however: hindsight is a wonderful thing, but in the 1970s I'm not sure that anyone could have predicted that the old station and post office would still be unloved islands in a sea of relative prosperity, and the question 'What shall we do about the Coal Exchange?' remain unanswered.

For many years, the Pier Head was a natural focal point: the trams stopped there, untold numbers of people took the paddle steamer for a day out—maybe a holiday. The dry docks nearby attracted ships needing attention, leading to urgent bursts of work for skilled, highly-paid tradesmen; and regular dredging took place to make sure ships could get to all the places they needed to call at.

Bit by bit, things changed: investment and maintenance dried up and deposits of sticky brown silt clogged the approaches and channels. The silting was condemned as signalling the end for a big slice of traditional maritime activity in Cardiff, and as an eyesore for visitors at low tide. But to make life even more interesting it was deemed that the mud and its contents was just what wading birds like best for breakfast (and most of their other meals apparently) and couldn't just be washed away and disposed of. After a good deal of debate, the barrage was built to give consistently high water levels—so concealing a range of sins - and alternative mud is available for the birds just beyond Newport. The barrage has been followed by a lot of less spectacular civil engineering work, and extensive investments in all the wine bars and the rest which I have mentioned already. All I can say that you had to be fairly visionary in the 1970s to see all of this lot heading towards you.

Images of Wales

Housing in South Cardiff: Cardiff was part-way through various slum clearance programmes. What remains can be highly sought-after.

Older housing was certainly unpopular for a while, but much is now both valued and valuable. The same cannot be said for the corner shops and other local retail businesses—no matter how colourful their owners and customers. Fundamental changes to the way people did their shopping transferred families' spending to supermarkets. Convenience to home mattered less and less with booming numbers of cars and home freezers.

Those of you who know Cardiff will appreciate that there is well over a mile between the City Centre itself and the Docks. The plans developed and (partly) implemented by the Cardiff Bay Development Corporation expressed a confident expectation that this gap would rapidly be superseded by a stream of modern development along a sparkling 'Corniche'. I suppose this gap is now less of an issue than it once was, but it still seems inescapable that the City Centre and the Bay were simply built too far apart to allow easy, routine contact.

In the 1970s various derelict sites emphasise an apparent lack of much interest in what went on south of the main railway line, but they made interesting places to play around in.

Shops in south and central Cardiff: far from easy to compete with large chains—no matter how entertaining and colourful the management.

There were still traces of specialist heavy
engineers, mainly linked to the maritime
past. Dry docks, people who could sort out
problems with propellers; specialist forges and
foundries. It was not just declining markets:
for some it was clear that the value of the
site had risen significantly, with inevitable
temptations to cash in.

Heavy industry: the Norwegian church (see previous page) has now been relocated to a prominent site on the waterfront in the redeveloped Cardiff Bay. In 1970 its old site was closer to cranes and other machines for dealing with big lumps of metal. But they've gone altogether.

In the gap between the City Centre and the Docks. Better now, but still a concern. In the 1970s nobody seemed very bothered. So lads wandered around, as they do; litter was plentiful—amongst luxuriant weed growth.

Left The 'Brains Beer' advert subsequently reappeared with a 'retro' style to promote the well-known Cardiff-made beverages. For many years you could smell the St Mary Street brewery fairly widely around the City Centre. Not a particularly good way of promoting the products in many peoples' estimation.

I have included this gable end, with its nasty graffiti, as a reminder. I have worked, socialised and worshipped with people from all sorts of ethnic backgrounds in central Cardiff, and feel greatly enriched by it. I do not think you would see this sort of message sprayed up today, but it is worth remembering that we should not take these things for granted.

Below When an area got run-down, despite brave talk of strong communities and important local traditions, it could certainly look gloomy. And at the time these was no certainty that the capital City of Wales, without the traditional income generators in the docks and steelworks, had much of a future at all.

Interestingly, there has been time for a fairly substantial Cardiff Bay public building to be designed, built, opened, run for a while, then closed and demolished. I refer of course to the Welsh Industrial and Maritime Museum, open between 1977–98. There were large machines from the past prone to hiss and clank in interesting ways; there was a frisson of danger as children climbed around the grubby old steam tug Sea Alarm; and there were various other artefacts which kept our children (and me) diverted for ages at minimal cost.

Then all of a sudden the National Museum had a new strategy and the WIMM wasn't part of it. Some material has gone to Swansea and the museum on the waterfront there; some is stored; the poor old Sea Alarm has undergone the most radical transformation of all: from being a valued relic of a proud past to scrapped and melted down.

Right and below Welsh Industrial and Maritime Museum.

Above Crossing the north-south
divide. Bridges across the main
railway line.

Left These are the clean lines of ss
King George V, an elegant steam
turbine, screw-driven vessel retired
from the Clyde in 1974 and hanging
about in Cardiff's dry docks for
some years afterwards prior, it was
thought, to a change of careers as a
floating restaurant. A careless spark,
a flame, a major blaze and this was
what was left . By now, a date with
the breakers had become the only
viable action.

Ferry Road didn't attract too many visitors—it didn't feature in the tourism promotions, and there were very big dogs at a couple of the scrap yards. But there were glorious textures and shapes, if you had an eye for these sorts of things, and a bit of imagination, in the careworn equipment there .

A bus burning by the East Dock: at least it doesn't seem to be interfering with the fishing.

The traditional scale and style of the central shopping area had its fans, but the trends were all in other directions.

In other parts of the City housing became run-down—like these once-grand properties in Newport Road. Many (including these) escaped demolition and, when sensitively restored, can be highly sought after, with their high ceilings, proximity to the central area, and general aura.

Above Rover Way: named for the motor factory opened just after the war with high hopes for industrial diversification and exports through the docks. This was not to happen, but Rover Way became a crucial route for heavy goods vehicles, and HGV drivers need caffs....

Below Increasingly unused docks; unloved, abandoned Morris Minor.

We'll end this section with a quick look at some of the ways in which people spent their leisure time. Traditional cinemas didn't do so well in an era when colour tvs at home became increasingly popular - but the industry was able to fight back with multiplexes and, generally speaking, a better offer overall. The traditional fairs probably looked like they were from a bygone age, not something with much of a future, but later evolved into much larger events around Cathays Park in the winter and summer festivals. Change in Cardiff parks has been more subtle, but there's a lot more attention to health and safety around the swings, and the ducks are left in a bit more peace in Roath Park because you can't row around the islands these days.

Boating on Roath Park Lake. Open for swimming for many years, but boats only in the 1970s—at least you could go round the islands then.

Above The County cinema closed.

Below Fairs kept coming, but the big takeovers of Cathays Park were a long way in the future.

And plenty of parks and swings—then as now.

three

Coal, Iron and Steel

In 1970 the coal and steel industries employed many tens of thousands of people in Wales, but if you lived in large swathes of the nation you could be entitled to say that it did not really affect you. That is misleading to a degree: to begin with, coal has been mined over the years in much wider areas than you might think—across much of Pembrokeshire, for example—and before coal (converted to coke) became part of the normal blast furnace load, the job was done by charcoal. It took a large number of trees to make a ton of iron, so there were many sites for furnaces around what is now very definitely rural Wales—Tintern being one example.

I say this partly to avoid the dangers of saying that the coal and the iron and steel industries affected just a handful of areas in North East and South East Wales— thereby, perhaps, marginalising what were crucial drivers of the whole Welsh economy for decades. Another important point—to me at least—is the impact these industries have had on what is now much-admired countryside. There are many examples across Wales where interesting green hills are really former spoil heaps, not just courtesy of Mother Nature. In many ways this is what lies behind the landscape around Blaenavon—a World Heritage Site, after all.

As a former British Steel Corporation employee, I have decided to look at this industry first. Looking back, technological change has been the dominant factor behind most of the changes, but that has come hand in hand with market changes like the global trading of both raw materials and finished products.

Today, most steel tonnage throughout the world arises through hugely productive basic oxygen steelmaking plants using continuous casting techniques to produce billets and slabs direct. Scrap is dealt with through electric arc plants, and Cardiff secured one of these after the demise of East Moors, but it hardly compared in employment terms. About one tenth of the East Moors workforce was needed to deliver about half the tonnage of steel.

In 1970, Wales had many kinds of steelworks. Major investments at Llanwern and Port Talbot were bringing the new technologies there as the basis for fairly large,

Spoil heaps on their way to becoming landscape. If left long enough, they can become 'features' but most have been obliterated. Sometimes there were safety fears, following the Aberfan disaster. But there also seems to be a particular view of what Wales should look like: green and 'natural' in areas with rather different—but proud—traditions.

At its worst, though, coal mining isn't pretty.

East Moors: despite an active campaign to stave off closure, Cardiff seems to have generated plenty of other jobs—though not necessarily paying so well.

The black arts of the open hearth process. All about knowing what to shovel in, and when.

fairly modern plants there (though not quite to Japanese scales); there were electric arc plants for special steels (like Panteg); and a wide range of mills for rolling complex sections and plating. The black arts of the open hearth process were widely practiced in Wales, however, as in the rest of he UK.

Many management processes were as arcane and outmoded as the technology they controlled, but I felt afterwards that I had learned a lot during my time in this gritty, financially-underperforming environment. Like what to do when the senior figure you are making a presentation to falls heavily asleep: answer—press on anyway, for when he wakes up his likeliest response will be 'that sounds alright—go ahead'.

Then there is the question of who might just have an idea about what's going wrong in a noisy, hot and very dirty environment: answer, the crane drivers. They don't just read the *Daily Mirror* and drink tea, you know—they look down and observe strange things going on.

I think I also learned the value of keeping your eyes and ears open. One of the re-heating furnaces was said to have a problem with red-hot bars climbing over each other as they were 'walked' from one side to the other. You cannot put a marker on something getting heated to these temperatures, so the first anyone would know that bars might have got out of order was when they had been rolled into the wrong product.

Working with hot bars. Not much evidence of protective clothing: shirt sleeves seem enough in temperatures closer to a Spanish beach than a grey day in South Wales.

Well maybe. But I began to suspect that the official records of how furnaces were being loaded were being supplemented from handwritten data on a grey card tucked behind a pipe.

When I overheard a furtive phone call with the phrase 'Is it a 3 or an 8?' I felt I had an idea of what might be going on. Not a good idea to confront long-serving and wily foremen, however; better to offer them a simpler new system, and get rid of the grey card and the pipe.

East Moors in Cardiff had been built between the Wars, in effect to replace the Dowlais plant in Merthyr with access to imported iron ore, no longer available in sufficient quantities in the way it had been when Merthyr was the foremost iron making centre in the world.

By the 1970s East Moors was outmoded; too small for BSC's vision of vast, Japanese-style plants, and it eventually closed in 1978. The predictions of massive problems in the local economy from the loss of 4,500 jobs were, by and large, found to be too pessimistic, for Cardiff had, by now, embarked on a transformation to become very clearly the pre-eminent commercial, administrative and retail centre in Wales.

Ebbw Vale was a bit different. In the 1930s claims were made that this was the largest steelworks in the world, high up in the Monmouthshire hills. Consett's

Wave-ground billets: a premium product, produced from the highest spec steel—provided the systems were working properly.

East Moors dominated the local community in several ways but not for much longer.

Above and overleaf The drama of Ebbw Vale. Once the largest steelworks in the world (probably)—crammed into a fairly tight valley, high up in the Monmouthshire hills.

In its time, the Ebbw Vale works sent its products all over the world; for many years, the Ebbw Vale rugby team was highly competitive, a force to be reckoned with across Wales; the spire of Christ Church is amongst the finest in the whole of the valleys. There are actually two Ebbw rivers and hence two separate valleys (they meet at Aberbeeg). For some local people there's a definite reluctance to travel from one to the other, and maybe a view that 'investment only goes to the other lot'. Ah well; it's by no means the only place where this sort of thing happens.

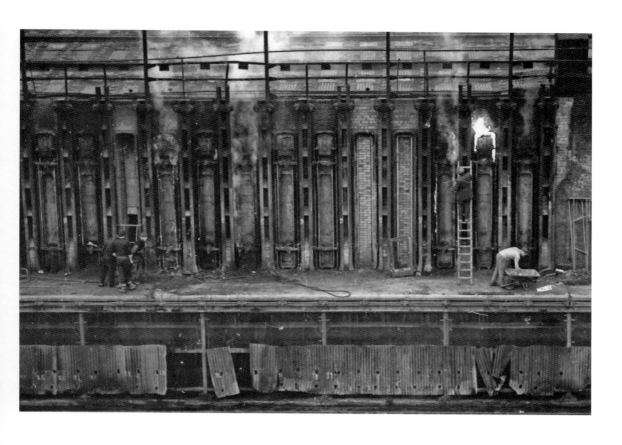

position in County Durham was similar, established to take advantage of once-plentiful local iron ore, coal and limestone. When these dwindled, imports had to be lugged by train up some big hills to keep the furnaces running.

When the works closed, also in the 1970s, intense campaigning was rewarded by major investment in a tinplate works—but this was to close in 2002. Despite adventures like the 1992 Garden Festival and the subsequent promotion of shopping and new housing, Ebbw Vale does not yet seem to have found the new role it needs in an era without all those steelworks jobs. And so to coal.

I did not have the same relationship with the coal industry. In another book I have written about how much I enjoyed the NCB's promotional event for 'bright lads who wanted to be part of Britain's modern mining industry'. Like virtually everyone else on the trip, I treated it as an entertaining couple of days out, with no question of signing up for a job underground. Anyway, I was too tall to walk around without banging my head into all sorts of random kit which seemed to line the roadways.

Coal stockpiles: dull, black and boring from so many perspectives, but potentially of great strategic importance. There was a widely held theory that miners had the best chance of winning any industrial action if they walked out before Christmas, preferably in a year where there were low levels of' coal stocks at the power stations. In 1984, industrial action started in March; there were record levels of stocks at the power stations .

I did not find it easy to capture the essence of mining in Wales. Broadly speaking, the pits operated five days per week, and that was when I was supposed to be at work myself. Most of what I have got is fairly bland shots of headgear set against terraced housing, or with pigeons, or anything else which seemed to be around. I am well aware that if you work in the industry, headgear is distinctive and often triggers strong memories for those who have worked at particular pits. I struggled, though, to see much difference. But, whilst commonplace images from the 1970s they may be, there are very few opportunities to capture anything remotely similar these days.

Images of Wales

That was not quite the end of my underground experience, however. One Saturday afternoon, while hunting the last few steam railway engines operated by the NCB in South Wales, I was with a friend who drew my attention to the distinctive sound of a steam winding engine chuffing away to support some maintenance work or other. The man in charge of it was proud of this relatively elderly, but shiny and effective machinery and not only demonstrated it for us, but offered us a ride to pit-bottom. So if I ever try to write up my list of steam-powered trips (unlikely, I admit) I will have to find a way of including a hundred fathoms or so of very smooth and rapid vertical travel.

At this point I must offer a sincere apology to my friends in North Wales. I am very well aware of the coal and steel industries here—it is just that I haven't any photographs which are suitable for inclusion here. I am particularly impressed that there is still the comforting site of a large colliery spoil heap as you approach Wrexham along the A483; to my mind, South Wales has been a bit too quick to obliterate these once-familiar landscape features.

A couple of details; first, the amounts of coal gathered by local people from tips for their own use in Wales were small by comparison with what the sea coalers of the North East gathered—at least that seemed to be the case, although it is a topic without much in the way of official statistics. It happened to some extent, though—more so, I suspect, when the miners were striking.

And a quick reference to electricity. Most coal, latterly, has gone to power stations for power generation. The steel industry is more complex with most integrated steelworks being both users and generators; electric arc plants tend to be just users, though very big users as you see in the awesome moments when the arc is struck. So, both of these industries are closely associated with a lot of cables.

But last of all of all, a quick trip to Abercwmboi (between Mountain Ash and Aberdare) and the Phurnacite plant—now long demolished. Phurnacite was a 'patent fuel'—flattened egg-shaped pellets made mainly from coal dust at a fuming monster of a plant, which seemed to have killed off every living thing for some distance around. It regularly attracted the ire of the environmental movement, as well as TV crews looking for something which could, with a bit of filtering and choice of viewpoint, match many people's imaginings of hell. A bit unfair, maybe; the bleak dead trees had, I suspect, died because the tipped land they grew in had caught fire—like a lot of other spoil heaps over the years. The plant itself was not pretty, but maybe no worse than a lot of coke and gas works around the country.

Opposite above Driving the steam winder; delivering a few hundred feet of vertical travel very swiftly and smoothly.

Opposite below Now coal mining was not just down to the NCB in the 1970s, nor is it totally dominated by British Coal now. Open-casting remains controversial but can certainly deliver big tonnages when approved. Private mines are small, often fairly untidy, but have the flexibility to react to the price of coal and changes in wider demand patterns. This is the Blaencuffin mine (sometimes Blaen Kyffin or other versions) near Abertillery.

Right Collecting coal from the tip.

Below Power lines near Ebbw Vale.

Inset A very brief mention for opencast mining. Never popular, but highly profitable, it goes on to this day, well after deep-mining has ceased.

The Phurnacite works at Abercwnboi, with dead trees. But were they dead because of the fumes spewing from the patent fuel works, or was the ground they grew in—like much other colliery waste—on fire because of the coal it contained?

The Phurnacite plant, with dead trees and a family outing.

four

The Coast

Maybe things have been a bit serious and even gloomy so far, but there were plenty of opportunities for having fun in the 1970s—as there are now—not least along the extensive Welsh coast. There are some long, straight beaches (like Pendine) but many more stretches are distinctly crinkly, with lots of inlets and outcrops to increase the length of the actual coastline, and provide variety and interest.

Inevitably the 1970s saw challenges. The basic mass-market tourism 'offer' emerged in the late nineteenth and early twentieth centuries. The resorts along the North Wales coast in particular prospered as workers from the English Midlands and North West took their annual holidays at the nearest stretch of coast—good news for Rhyl, Colwyn Bay and their neighbours. There were some parallels in South Wales at Barry and Porthcawl. The trouble was that tastes were changing, horizons were broadening, and package tour offers multiplied.

Tourism was—and to some extent still is—focused on the traditional summer months. In truth, the winter months might not give the warmest welcome.

Yet there were some signs of tourism growth. The little trains in the north flourished; so did Portmeirion, particularly after the 17 episodes of *The Prisoner* in 1967–68. The castles drew visitors, and the less developed, naturally rugged coastline attracted some, particularly the better-off, less bucket-and-spade sort of holidaymaker. The basic message seemed to be that something unique and of high quality had a chance; a lot of traditional stuff was going to struggle.

But at the same time fields full of static caravans proliferated and costs could be cut to the bone—if you needed them to be. It has been an evolving, changing picture, but one way or another, lots of people came to the seaside in Wales in 1970, and they still do. It's just that some locations did better than others.

Take Barry for instance, there was still the infrastructure that went with countless thousands of visitors—both coming for the day and staying for longer at Butlin's. The palm trees in the gardens leading to the beach, the cafés and the funfair were all there, but starting to look a bit tired.

Above The Welsh coast: crinkly, with all those bays and headlands.

Left The seaside brings out cameras and photographers in droves—particularly if the sun is shining. I tended to find more to photograph on a grey day in Ebbw Vale, say, where you might have to wait for years before seeing anyone else with a camera. This photograph could have been taken at any time in the post-war era—up to the invention of the picture taking mobile phone and the iPad, that is. But fortunately for the purposes of this book, there can be only one decade when gentlemen staying in Tenby would turn themselves out in flared trousers like those.

The traditional basics; water, sand, fishing, trips round the bay, chips. Lots of things to do—well quite a lot, anyway.

But by the 1970s this was no longer quite enough for some of the customers. Numbers of visitors were down and some of the infrastructure needed attention.

Below Different kinds of seaside—the Heritage Coast near Southerndown.

The coast in winter. Better get wrapped up … and get ready to make your own amusements, preferably in other ways than carving more initials in the overcrowded woodwork.

Above The attractions of the rugged, less developed coastline—in this case the flooded quarry aka The Blue Lagoon in north Pembrokeshire.

Right Port Meirion; unique, world famous—but all too few of this kind of attraction in Wales, unfortunately.

Above Striking views when the hills come down to meet the sea.

Below And the lure of the static caravan has not seemed to decline. This picture was taken from a speeding train on the North Wales Coast line, hence the (deliberate) blurring.

Along with some of the resorts along the North Wales coast, Barry seemed to be hit hardest by new tastes and trends in holidaymaking. With the fine beach and the cafés and amusements, Barry still attracted large numbers of day visitors in the 1970s—and does still—but there was clear evidence of decline. The sand and sea remained good, but a number of businesses ceased trading and the general spirit and brash energy of the place seemed to fade a bit. I don't think it was just me getting older: other people noticed it too, and really it was just part of industry-wide trends in the UK, a bit like coal and steel.

The funfair; the scenic railway starting to look a bit tired and the Ghost Train looked less ghostly.

Times were changing. People did still come, in cars and coaches, and the regular little diesel trains brought a few. But there were not the big numbers on special trains pouring out of the Valleys, with people packed into coaches hauled by a freight engine on its 'days off' from weekday coal shifting.

The Butlin's Holiday Camp was first sold on, then closed altogether as this more regimented approach to having fun started to lose its allure. Later (it didn't appear until January 1980) the BBC's *Hi-de-hi* comedy series probably didn't help, and maybe the tired old jokes about supposed resemblances to Colditz really did start to have an effect.

Of course for many of us in the 1970s Barry meant something else altogether. Woodham's scrap yard held dozens of steam railway engines for many years—most ending up being 'rescued' and rebuilt for service on preserved lines across the nation. The scrapyard also provided a useful short-cut between the town and the beach at Barry Island, so the rusting boilers and frames were visited by people with the utmost interest in steam technology, and people with none at all

Further along the coast, Aberavon has three miles of fine beaches, good parking and indoor recreation facilities for when the weather is poor. It is also part of Port Talbot which has a great big steelworks and the tidal harbour through which pass vast quantities of iron ore and coal on their way to the furnaces.

For decades there have been efforts to promote the beach bit to visitors (as 'The Afan Lido') and downplay the rest. It is very much like Redcar in the North East—it depends which way you look, and how important you think it is to avoid heavy industry in the background to your antics on the beach.

Now I simply cannot make this a comprehensive review of Welsh coastal resorts in the 1970s. There is not the space, and I do not have the material. We had family holidays or weekends on Lleyn, Anglesey, Menai, Tenby, North Pembrokeshire, and Cardigan Bay. I spent my honeymoon in Barmouth, and took countless day trips to Gower, Porthcawl, Southerndown and the rest. As the 1970s wore on, I found I was taking more and more photos of my children, many fewer of the localities they were in.

Above It was difficult to resist the temptation to portray the holiday camp visitors as somehow imprisoned. In practice, those I spoke to were enjoying themselves well enough.

Below The quick way to the beach, through the scrapyard.

The Afan Lido/Port Talbot. Nice beach, pity about the steelworks. The 'Locals Only' message is a bit of a mystery, I do not recall much evidence of any other kind of visitor.

I have never seen the golden sands and imaginative concrete at the Afan Lido heavily used. At the time I saw her, the image of the abandoned doll in the car park mud seemed to sum up a lot of what was going on there. Things were a bit different at Penarth despite its unprepossessing shingle beach (apparently there were sands here until quite recently, the disappearance being due to natural forces rather than the dredgers on the sandbanks, so the official assessments have it: thank goodness for that!).

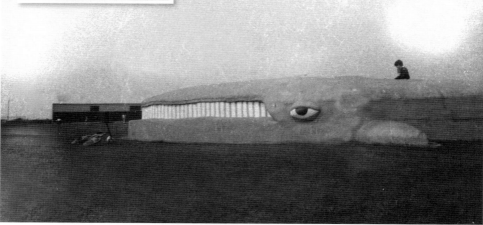

One of the great attractions on some of the Welsh coasts (like here at Tenby) is the way that sea, sand, rocks and development sit close-by, and generally make everything that bit more interesting.

There's more to Tenby than beaches and rocks, though. On first appearance little has changed over the years, but some cobwebs are said to have been blown away by, for example the arrival of 'hen parties' (sorry, I have no photos).

Gestures towards the north; first, Barmouth. The Bridge still has 'British Railways' signs. Perhaps local managers knew that British Rail wouldn't last.

Beach huts beside the Fairborne Railway.

Enticing kiosks—out of season.

A final reminder of the Welsh coast; good beaches, sometimes close to dramatic scenery, and can be quiet for most of the year.

five

Transport

When I first came to Wales in 1969 it was a great delight to find that the NCB in South Wales still had steam railway engines—just about—if you looked carefully and I tracked down as many as I could.

It was a while before I had a car—and when I did get one it lacked some of the basics in terms of comfort and reliability. Worse, I was a bit tied up during the working week. You can cut a lecture as a student, and if paid by the hour, on some jobs anyway, you can negotiate odd bits of time off. A regular salary closes most of these doors.

It was therefore mainly at weekends that I was scurrying around the last few tank engines in the Valleys—often cold and dead in sidings (the locomotives that is) but sometimes snug in comfy little sheds—all within not many miles of the crucial efforts of Trevithick on the Penydarren tramroad all those years ago.

The preserved narrow-gauge lines in North Wales were—and are—wonderful in the extreme. Because this is a book focusing on wider social and economic changes, so I've only included a reminder of when the Vale of Rheidol locomotives sported the British Rail logo, and some styles in mid-1970s wet gear.

If you live in South Wales and have business to attend to in the North or West, it is always tempting to arrange things so that you can fit in a trip on the Festiniog, say, or the Vale of Rheidol. But it's not always straightforward. If you are the only person in a dark business suit on the train, people can take it into their heads that you have some standing in the organisation and can either provide detailed information, or influence operational decisions, like time to wander around at intermediate stations. If it looks as if I'll have to share a train with a couple of coach-loads of Wallace Arnold's older female customers again, I think I'll try to talk my way into the guard's van.

There was much more to transportation than railways in the 1970s and the real winners were mainly road-based—cars, trucks and buses becoming increasingly dominant. I say 'mainly' only because air travel was doing well too; I have no photographs to illustrate the point, but the memory of being shoehorned into a cramped

BAC 1-11 on a cheap package holiday remains with me. The Severn Bridge had opened in 1966, but the M4 was creeping westwards only fitfully, and some of the other major roads were poor to say the least. If you think the A470 is a bad road now, just think of it when Cardiff to Merthyr took around an hour, and required negotiating delivery lorries and narrow carriageways built for horses and carts, not the dynamic luxury of the Triumph Herald.

I have included some images of local stations for several reasons; first, nice touches from the past remained in glass and ironwork, but also to emphasise how run-down and generally horrible many Valley facilities had become. Things are a bit better now, but mainly through demolition rather than attempting to make good the best of the past.

These days, it all makes for a busy but unlovely operation. It is very difficult to get enthusiastic about the 4-wheel 'Pacers' for example—which were, after all, largely put together from Leyland bus parts—almost a decade after the end of their intended 20 year working life. There is talk of electrification… starting by 2019… I suppose you never know…

Of course Wales retained national—perhaps international—status in the 1970s through the steam engines at Woodham's scrapyard in Barry. Officially due to be cut up and melted down, almost all were 'rescued' and can be seen on preserved lines and specials across the nation.

And finally let's not forget travelling on water. *Waverley* (and *Balmoral*) have kept alive the opportunity of cruising up and down the Bristol Channel. Several canals remain in use, and even when closed, people were quick to see the potential for walking and cycling.

This probably does not do justice to walking, cycling, bus travel and pony trekking. I tried them all in the 1970s (well, just once in the case of pony trekking). I have no pictures, and few nostalgic feelings to draw on. I will say, though, that when I was looking through the pictures of buses being scrapped I was briefly back in a world of drivers grinding gears as they slowly changed up and down, an upstairs cabin nearly solid with tobacco smoke, bus conductresses who seemed to have seen a bit of life, and open platforms guarded by said conductresses to stop you nipping on and off at the lights. Ahhh!

A pair of saddle tanks; cold now, but they've been working recently. Not for much longer, I fear.

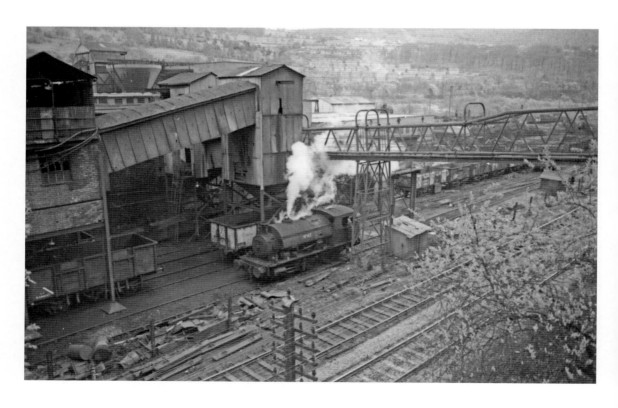

Just occasionally, there was some serious shunting to do, with a steam engine. Not many years before, it's doubtful if enthusiasts would take any interest at all in these utterly mundane tasks. Now that steam had gone from British Rail, and was going fast everywhere else, these humble tank engines received admiring visitors from far and wide.

Not necessarily the tidiest examples of engineering excellence, but delivering an effective service for many years. The familiar outline of an ex-GWR pannier tank is prominent, it seemed that 'worn out' for mainline work meant 'plenty of life left in her' for industrial applications.

The Vale of Rheidol, with BR logo.

The old British Railways crest on a once-green tender survives—just about—into an era of British Rail, the uniform blue livery, and the orange double-arrow logo.

Diesels on the main line. Like it or not, that was all you were going to get.

The Talylyn with Wellies.

I never saw a 'Castle' in routine main line service, so it's a delight to see them occasionally out and about. But it's a pale reflection of the way things used to be.

Roads were improving—but filling up—all the time. The (first) Severn Bridge was still something of a marvel. The A470 was slightly improved from time to time. The excuse for doing little to improve north–south links has always been 'hardly anybody uses them'. One reason why they are little-used is, to my mind, the lousy state of the roads. The news that 'Jesus Saves' was doubtless a comfort to many travellers, but in terms of time bulldozers and tarmac lorries could have led to useful savings too.

The railways had long experience of advertising, promotional fares, press relations and other marketing techniques. How this all worked out in practice varied: adverts for weekend deals and cheap returns to Bristol at Bute Road in Cardiff had probably once been reasonably clear, providing potentially useful information. They are now a bit grubby, and the evidence that the 70p cost figure has recently been covered by something else doesn't necessarily inspire confidence. At Pontypridd, however, I find it impossible to guess the message intended to be conveyed by this interesting combination of chalked-up train times and photograph of a scared-looking young lady.

Echoes of a more graceful, maybe more stylish era in the detailing of some fairly unloved stations (including Grangetown, on the Penarth line). The TVR initials cast into various items of ironwork recall the Taff Vale Railway, absorbed into the GWR in 1923.

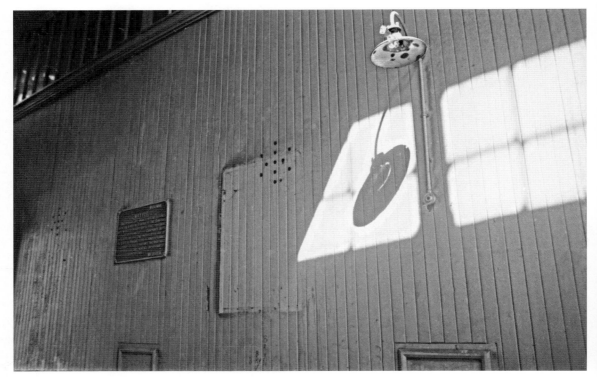

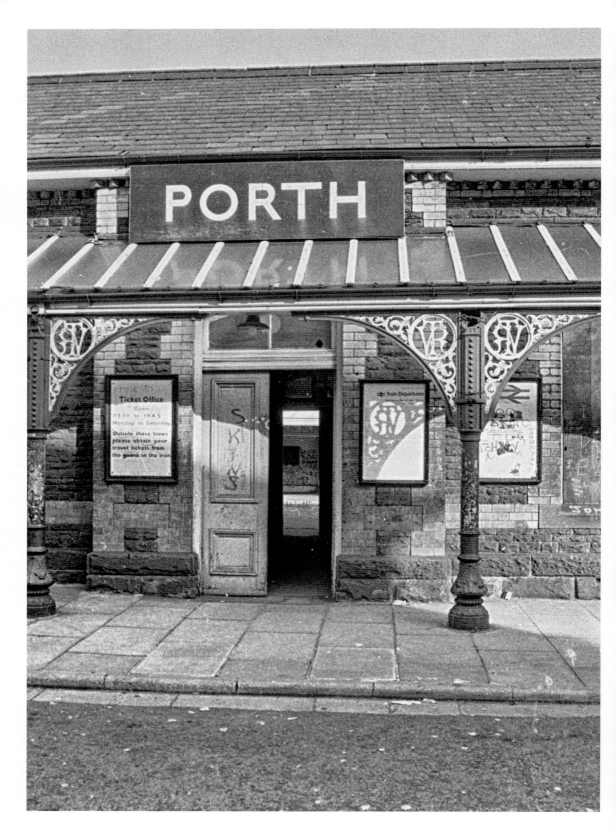

90   *Images of Wales*

Things got a lot worse once cheap aerosols became available. Where are Titch and Andy now? Bank managers? In gaol? Both?

Woodham's yard at Barry.

A gesture towards cycling. By no means as popular recreationally as it is now, without much of the competitive British success which came later. A lot of cyclists simply hadn't got a car, and cycled to places because they hadn't a better option. But this looks like a competitive enough roadrace, through the streets of Cardiff.

Paddle steamer *Waverley*, during regular seasonal visits.

Canals; active and re-used for leisure purposes.

six

The Valleys

I first spent time in the Welsh Valleys thanks to rugby. I thought I had probably played enough at school and college to last me and took a season off, but then the general chatter about the oval ball game in Wales drew me in, and lacking fitness, training and any sort of preparation, I had boots on and was playing. Welsh teams are frequently short of players. For a while one well-known club struggled to get bus drivers for away fixtures: they were fed up with being squeezed into someone else's kit and playing on the wing.

Most of the towns and villages in the Valleys were built in a hurry in the nineteenth century to house workers at the local pit. The houses had to be fitted in where space was not needed for the river, pit, railway, tips and the other necessities of the coal trade. When the pits closed you might have expected these essentially small, low-specification dwellings to follow. But there have been grants to keep the housing in good shape and I have lost count of people who've told me 'they wouldn't live anywhere else'. A big contrast with County Durham, then, where those ('Category D') former mining villages thought not to have a viable future were starved of resources and, in effect, closed down.

Images of the Valleys on an average day. Quite interesting, but a bit ho-hum. Grey slate roofs can appear, well, overwhelmingly grey; it's heresy for anyone local, but for the passing photographer one town starts to look similar to the next.

My first game of rugby in Wales was against one of the Monmouthshire valley sides, which we can call for illustrative purposes Fleur-de-lis ('C'mon Flower!'). It took me about five minutes to confirm some of the distinctive features of Welsh rugby—short but sturdy forwards with intuitive organisation and a good set of legal and quasi-legal technical skills. I was significantly taller than the opposition lineout jumpers and looked forward to a productive afternoon. I did not show my hand straight away, but neither did the opposition. After a bit I got airborne a couple of times and nothing harmful happened, but then in a flurry of choreographed action I found myself on the ground, and by a process of personal examination inferred the likelihood of two significant punches and a well-directed boot. 'Hmm', I thought, 'point taken'.

That's just the way it is; not necessarily dirty, but committed and competitive. Off the pitch too. Being from the north of England I hadn't much experience of, nor empathy with Home Counties banter from chaps on the touchline. I was better used to partisan moaning to the ref and silence from the home fans if we scored. But it still took a while to adjust to the comments from a partisan posse of unmarried mothers braving rain blown horizontally by a cold, remorseless wind that sought out any thoughts of smart handling movements and destroyed them.

This is all beside the main point, which is to introduce some images of the Valleys in the 1970s.

I have never found the Valleys particularly easy to photograph. People who live there will have a lot to say about their local community and the street where they live. But visually there is a tendency for one valley to look a bit like others, as the terrace houses snake along, squeezed into any spare piece of land along the valley bottom.

One response to the worry that 'It all looks the same' was one I'd used a lot in the North of England; bad weather. A bit of fog or snow made things look a lot more interesting. You must not think, from my eager use of this additional visual dimension that it snows a lot in the Valleys, or is usually foggy: just the reverse.

Rare, but maybe photographically most exciting of all was fog, concealing everything not close by, and adding depth and mystery. Not easy to work with though; too thick and you can' see anything at all. And driving around a complex, unfamiliar area in poor visibility isn't entirely to be recommended.

As ever, there were all sorts of details in the Valleys to catch the attention of the inquisitive photographer—varying from pigeons in flight to drinking establishments which sheltered under the railway arches.

It is sometimes easy to forget about the flat land between the Valleys, and at their northern edges—the 'Heads of the Valleys'. This flat land has caught the eye of factory developers, and sometimes Councils who wanted to build houses, like at Penrhys in the Rhondda. Elsewhere, interesting less formal developments have sprung up—but you have to be sure they can stand up to strong winds and driving rain.

But with a bit of snow added, the Valleys became more interesting altogether. Little details are picked out, the distinctive features become more obvious.

Left Quite a few playgrounds and sports fields stand out as you travel around industrial South Wales. The Valleys have a proud sporting tradition; football, rugby, darts, snooker—you name it; unfortunately healthy forces are confronted by illnesses from working in mines and heavy industry, and 'lifestyle' choices.

Below Not every house was desired, loved and cherished. Some were knocked down, others fell down—but these were in the minority within the housing stock as a whole.

Below Betting offices became legal in 1961, but were not entirely welcomed by some communities, and this one seems to have been banished to a lonely spot in the snow.

It was not just snow and fog which brought out different facets of the Valleys. Strong evening sunlight is good for picking out details, but you have to be careful. The sun does not reach the communities along the bottom of narrow valleys from early afternoon onwards in winter. All may look sharp and enticing as you drive along the M4 at lunchtime; you could have only deep shadows after you turn off.

Sometimes houses, pits and spoil heaps did come closer together than maybe they should—the Aberfan disaster showed how dangerous this could be. Here there are tips in the foreground and tips in the background, with a lot of houses tucked in between, and a solitary car; it looks like a 1960s Singer Gazelle.

Pigeons in flight. Very different in all sorts of ways to the feral, urban scavenger, you can see racing pigeons in many industrial areas, and marvel at their homing skills. There can be a clash with people who have other priorities—like supporters of the Peregrine falcons slowly retaking their station as top avian predator (a pair has been nesting on Cardiff City Hall recently). Unfortunately, Peregrines may see a racing pigeon and think 'meal'.

There was (and is) all sorts of history tucked away. This unassuming iron bridge in the Clyddach Gorge is dated 1824, not so long after the use of this material was first achieved. I have included the second image with what looks like a luminous bat not because of any belief in the paranormal. It's got one or two people excited about ghostly figures, but the truth is that a gnat of some sort got trapped and flattened between two negatives.

Left 'Men only' signs were not uncommon for many years, but rapidly became history as the 1970s wore on.

Above The 'Third Class' sign has no political overtones; it just harks back to the way fares on the railways were structured for many years (it became Second Class in 1956).

The railway fulfils many functions, including keeping the rain out of the Railway Inn.

The Valley trains shift commuters, shoppers and the rest of us in our thousands. New rolling stock would be nice… sometime. The current fleet dates from the 1980s and I'd like to refer to it in nostalgic terms—but it's what you see every day.

Sports fields and playgrounds—plenty of exercise opportunities, but overall health statistics are not so good.

Shapes in the snow.

On the flat land building is easier—but it has to be proof against wind and driving rain.

Below An informal play area, at the end of the summer holidays.

The flat land at the Heads of the Valleys attracted very early industrial development—hence the World Heritage site at Blaenavon—but also 'enlightened' investment after the Second World War when there were aspirations to provide good quality jobs for the many men even then leaving the pits and the steelworks. The grandeur of these visions even extended to employing high-profile architects and ambitious civil engineers. Unfortunately, many of these grand ideas did not stand the test of time. This is the Dnlop factory at Brynmawr... Or rather, it was.

In most valleys, roads and houses and employment and social life—everything, really—is crammed into a narrow strip running along the bottom of the valley. Up on the hills in between is like a separate world—often windswept and dramatic, with sunken roads and a few well-aged trees bent over by the prevailing westerlies.

Archibald Hood was a Scottish mining engineer, a great force in Wales particularly when the pits in the Rhondda were being developed. Here his statue, for some reason painted in fading pastel shades, looks bleakly down on an area which has gone from minimal coal extraction, through a massive boom and vast mining activity, through to minimal coal extraction again.

I spent a lot of time trying to get an evening shot of smoking chimney stacks in a low sun in the Welsh valleys, and never really succeeded. Maybe it was never going to happen quite the way I wanted because Welsh coal typically has a low volatile content and doesn't produce much smoke in the first place. As the 1970s wore on, however, people were as likely to have gas central heating in the Welsh valleys as anywhere else, so the challenge was to get the best out of the wet rooftops and the perspective looking down the valleys.

And finally some details: pubs, 'Industrial Terrace' and a question I simply cannot address: how did it all smell?

Ambitious pub signs were, I suppose, just another form of advertising. Colourful wall paintings outside public lavatories came under the heading of 'art'.

And finally, a crucial question for all Labradors: What did it all smell like? The honest answer: I have absolutely no idea.

seven
More of South Wales

We have had a look at Cardiff, the Valleys and some of the coast of South Wales. There's plenty more, like the flatlands going up the estuary. There are towns like Chepstow and Caldicot, villages tucked away, and scattered housing between Cardiff and Newport. But a lot of the time it's quiet, natural, birds calling—that sort of thing.

There can be surprises; like a pair of working traction engines (technically ploughing engines, I suspect) cleaning up a creek in the 1980s. But the Welsh side has not seen as much development as the English side, and there's no parallel with, say, Severn Beach—briefly notable through the Adge Cutler Hawaiian-style record 'Aloha Severn Beach' (including the lines 'I'll meet my sweet in her finery Down by that oil refinery').

Cardiff and Newport are creeping inexorably closer, mainly with industrial development on the Newport side, housing from Cardiff. The 1970s saw plenty of change here, with Cardiff building the big estates of Llanedeyrn and Pentwyn, with St Mellons soon to follow.

New development is closing the gap between Cardiff and Newport all the time, but next to the estuary itself there is some sporadic development, but mainly rough grazing, birdsong, big skies— that sort of thing.

Occasional surprises, like a pair of working traction engines dredging in the Victorian way. Admittedly this was in the 1980s, though the technology goes back into the nineteenth century, but it worked. As they pulled a dredging bucket from side to side up came all that silt and estuarial sludge without the need for any person or any heavy plant to go on it—and risk expensive and dangerous sinkings.

Below Chepstow.

The edge of the Pentwyn development, new housing at Tongwynlais; some attempts to be friendly to nature.

A couple of images of Newport docks and Transporter Bridge; several people have told me the bridge is unique, the last of its kind, and so on. Unfortunately, I've heard similar comments from a couple of Middlesbrough people about their bridge too.

I struggled to make large parts of Newport look interesting, but given a favourable sky, it has its own particular charm.

The Taffs Well gorge must have been important strategically since the Ice Age—maybe even before that. Since the Industrial Revolution it has seen packhorses, canal boats, vast quantities of railway tracks, and who knows how many pairs of hobnailed boots trudge through. The 1970s were the era of the articulated lorry, however. Castell Coch stands above it all, a 19th-century folly constructed for the Marquis of Bute—said at the time to be the richest man in the world, thanks to all that coal streaming from the valleys.

The Butes weren't the only people to make a lot of money in South Wales: Lord Tredegar and his family did quite nicely out of a 'golden mile' of railway track over which traffic into Newport docks had to pass. Those days are long since gone, of course: the best days of this mighty tree on their Tredegar Park estate are probably behind it, too.

The M4 spread fitfully across South Wales. Its limitations—like big queues to get through the Newport tunnels—only really became apparent later on.

I did some voluntary work at Hensol hospital, out in the Vale of Glamorgan, in the early 1970s. Hensol is now the home for a smart spa hotel, amongst other things, and the concept of a secure place where people could be sent, perhaps for many decades, was swept away by the move to Care in the Community. One Sunday afternoon I took photos of everyone on one of the wards who wanted me to, and have included a handful here. There's a lot which could be said about how a big ward (at least 40 residentdnts) could function with only a couple of staff, but the patients themselves undertook a lot of the work and organised many of their own interests and leisure activities.

But this was classic institutional life—for good or ill. One memory I retain says a lot; Sunday afternoon TV was very popular ('Who's calling the Golden Shot?' and the rest) but in the 3-day week there was sometimes no power. Asking a group of men sitting in their usual seats why they were staring at a blank screen I got the answer 'You get into a routine here.' You did indeed.

This spread and overleaf Faces from Hensol.

The Neath Valley, once heavily industrialised, but now notable for waterfalls, trees and reclaimed canals.

Sculpture at Margam Country Park, the steelworks is just a couple of miles away.

To end with, more history; Ogmore castle—with horse.

eight

Churches and Chapels

In the past, religion has always been important in Wales. The Christian tradition encompasses St David and 20,000 saints said to be buried on Bardsey, through the Great Revivals, and on to the present day.

Recent decades have seen great changes to churches and chapels in Wales—with numbers dropping sharply overall, although new forms of ministry and witness have emerged too.

The 2011 Census, apparently, indicates that fully 30 per cent of adults in Wales describe themselves as having no religion but—at least in popular imagination—it wasn't always so. The image of everyone going to hear high oratory from a pulpit every Sunday, and singing in natural four-part harmony is doubtless overdone, but pretty well everywhere you go in Wales, there are churches and chapels—not necessarily open, but demonstrating the extent of faith (or at least religious observance) which was the norm not so long ago.

There have been many closures and many people have simply drifted away, but in terms of images there remains vast variety, and many examples of change—the sub-text for this book.

This is not, of course, any survey or systematic review and looks mainly at churches and chapels in their local context (for example rural or urban settings); but there are some interesting side-issues like the wonderful variety of materials used for their construction.

Country churches and chapels are often wonderful—maybe for several reasons. One year we were on holiday on the Lleyn peninsula during the time that R. S. Thomas, the famous poet, was vicar of Aberdaraon. We went to the morning service well aware that he had a reputation for being outspoken, and indeed critical of various aspects of life in Wales. In fact the experience was altogether different. St Hywen's church is close to the sea, and was flooded with light, picking up vases with the subtle colours of wild flowers taken from the local hedgerows. And the sometimes angry and astringent phrases from the poet? No sign at all, in a thoughtful, elegantly worded homily.

Christ Church Ebbw Vale—'The Cathedral of the Hills'.

Country churches and chapels, built by local people without much in the way of formal architectural input, have a peaceful, spiritual quality all their own. Betjeman has a phrase 'washed by prayer' which describe some of the appeal.

136   *Images of Wales*

Sometimes, delightful details.

Like similar buildings in other parts of the UK, churches and chapels are often locked these days, maybe because of the pain of past theft. That's a shame because what's inside can include anything from the complex and stylish to the work of pious but less sophisticated hands from the past.

Particularly in the rural areas, nature is usually close at hand; that can mean a steady fight to keep all that rain out; occasionally the sea plays a part.

Of course many churches and chapels are much more integrated into towns and villages. With Wales often providing raw materials for the industrial revolution only, the income retained in the coal mining, slate quarrying or metalworking communities might not be great. So these buildings represented not just one of the few places where people could meet and important things could take place, their funding required considerable self-sacrifice.

Travelling around Wales, it is never easy to predict the style of the religious buildings you'll come across—simple designs from local builders or classical features—towers, spires—or none.

Corrugated Iron has been the construction medium of choice for many churches, chapels, Sunday schools and ancillary buildings. Usually billed as 'temporary', many corrugated iron structures have had a long and useful life. In some, the reverberations from those hard surfaces could make the singing spectacular.

We have met the Norwegian Church in Cardiff already, but here are views from different angles. Demolished and rebuilt on a prominent site overlooking the waters of Cardiff Bay, questions might be asked about how much of the Norwegian Church's original structure actually made the trip, but I think that misses the point: visually it remains a good-looking building, made from low-cost materials, and it's clearly in the tradition of these churches, once a familiar and popular feature at several ports along the coast.

We have to face facts, however, and many hundreds of churches and chapels have closed, and continue to do so. That does not necessarily mean they lose a certain aura, however.

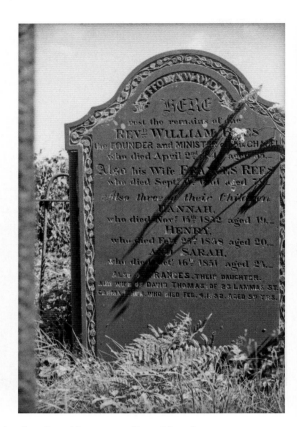

Nature may wish to play a part in the relationship between the church and its surroundings. Near the coast the sands may encroach. Many kinds of gravestone weather and give a home to lichens in engaging ways; Welsh slate holds out against these forces.

Churches and chapels in towns and villages; typically, very closely anchored to the communities they served.

Below Corrugated iron served churches well in Wales. It seems particularly appropriate to include this example from Merthyr, for many years the leading iron producing town in the world

Styles and designs—extraordinary variety.

The pious use of corrugated iron.

The Norwegian Church, Cardiff Bay in its original
location. Another big user of corrugated iron.

Other kinds of 'temporary' church buildings came
and (sometimes) went, including many timber
structures and what seems to be a former Nissen hut.

146   *Images of Wales*

'Praise ye the Lord!' Closed chapel, Thornhill.

Nant Gwrtheyrn, from the time when the whole village had been abandoned, not just the chapel.

Maybe it's just me, but I get a strong sense of witness even when churches have become 'abandoned' and roofless.

The picture for most churches and chapels in the 1970s was one of decline—but they were often the largest buildings in the locality and community life.

nine

North and West

I had plenty of opportunities to take more photographs in North and West Wales than I did in the 1970s. As well as holidays and visiting friends, I had meetings to go to and people to see there. But I also had a young family, and for work usually had to travel with other people, of a variety unlikely to welcome hanging around while I vanished for an hour with my camera. I have also included some material from the West and North in earlier chapters.

Enough excuses; let's make a start with some rural images.

In terms of acreage, most of Wales is, after all, based on agriculture rather than industry; if you travel from South Wales to North or West Wales, you will see plenty of greenery—and sheep.

Travelling from east to west in Wales is, generally, straightforward, with the M4 in the south, the A55 in the north and the A44 in the middle. North to south is a different matter. I have known otherwise respectable, decent people utter dreadful profanities at the sight of temporary traffic lights. If not at the first, then maybe at the twenty-first, for these important road safety features seem to come in packs, and if you have encountered one, you may confidently expect more. And woe betide anyone trying to press on after a delay; the police know about the temptation, and sometimes lie in wait.

It's an ill wind, though, and while waiting in line at a temporary traffic light on the A483 got the picture of the farmer (if that's what he is) striding through the rain—boots, gaiters, stout stick and all.

Mid Wales has fine small towns, amongst all that farmland and forestry. I tended to stop only briefly in the 1970s, but enjoyed the Tudor buildings and sense of traditional values in retailing and catering. Decimalisation took place in 1971, but in parts of Mid Wales it felt to me that you should still be working with half-crowns and ten-bob notes for several years afterwards.

As you get into North Wales the landscape gets distinctly rockier, and the hills more spectacular. The hillier bits attract even more rain than the flat bits.

Right Waiting for the sheep to go where the farmer wants them to. Despite the best efforts of man and dog, they want to explore the hedgerows rather than trot meekly along the highway from one field to the next.

Below Sheep safely gathered in; by far the best place for them, in my view.

Above Striding through the rain—boots, gaiters, stout stick and all.

Left God and mammon, or at least Calvinistic Methodism and the Coal and Lime Company

Right Tradition in retailing.

Below Pubs were having a tough time too. The Forest Arms has been the scene for determined efforts by local people to buy and re-open it—in a community which has recently lost its school and chapel. At the time I write this, their chances of success do not look good.

Rain gathers in lakes—natural and man-made. Water was not privatised until 1989, and controversy lingers about several aspects of water abstraction and intrusive reservoirs which benefit English cities, not Welsh communities. Maybe there are signs that the potential of these attractive stretches of fresh water is starting to be exploited, however; access is getting a bit easier, and numbers of centres and attractions steadily rising. In the 1970s there were rather more 'keep out' signs.

You can now walk beside some of the lakes, go fishing or boating on others, and enjoy the Llanberis Lake Railway or the delights of the Dinorwic pumped storage scheme. As ever, though, there are complications. The site at one end of the lake at Trawsfynydd is, after all, a former nuclear power station. Diving in flooded former slate quarries may be a lot of fun, but has led to a stream of fatalities as divers have become trapped in all that interesting debris down there.

There's a lot to see and do in North and West Wales, with a good stock of spectacular castles for those who like these things. But they don't tend to change much these days, so I've only included a token image as a reminder.

In large parts of North West Wales you just cannot ignore slate. The tips dominate the villages; vast, if mysterious, stone-built structures remain to show the effort and investment once needed by this unique industry. Networks of worn pathways now see the occasional Goretex-clad rambler, not the daily march of scores of hobnailed workers.

Unlike a coal spoil heap, say, which can grass-over fairly quickly, it takes a very long time before a haze of vegetation appears on a slate tip, so they remain black and dominant in a very distinctive way. Just occasionally, plants find sufficient nourishment (they could hardly be short of water) to claim a foothold and catch the eye in ways impossible in the lush green valleys.

Fairly slowly, some tourism potential started to emerge in the 1970s. The Dinorwic quarry closed in 1969 and the museum at Llanberis was formed in the workshops—giving the impression that the workers might be back at any minute.

By contrast with coal and slate, other mining and quarrying sometimes gets overlooked. But the Romans came looking for the gold; Parys mountain on Anglesey once dominated British copper production; and so it goes on. So here are some images, mainly from West Wales, and mainly now swept away.

One abandoned aftermath of quarrying has found a distinctive new life in Nant Gwrtheyrn, a centre promoting the Welsh language and culture, offering courses, holidays, and a wedding venue. You can also drive there now—something you could not do in the 1970s when the whole village remained empty and abandoned—but it was worth the walk one crystalline morning when we were staying not far away on Lleyn.

Quickly to Barmouth; we looked at its seaside aspect earlier. For some reason, the town itself seemed to have signs on any available surface for a while. The Nip-a-kof product is one of the few which completely defeats Google.

North Wales: rockier.

Lakes, both natural and the other kind. The flooded Dorothea slate quarry is a great attraction to divers; but they are prone to get caught on underwater obstructions and the fatalities have mounted.

Right Conifer planting changed many local views fundamentally; at worst, drab and dismal, at best, woodland makes a change from all those sheep across wet, cold uplands.

Below What makes the trees grow so well; the weather can be wonderful, but the average rainfall figures do not lie.

Above I forget this dog's name, but met him during a weekend in the Carmarthenshire hills. He seemed like a fine dog, totally monolingual—responding to the Welsh language only and shaking his tail sadly if addressed in English.

Below Jackdaws at Harlech castle.

Blaenau Festiniog.

Mysterious, beautifully crafted stone-built structures; silent paths; every so often, jewel-like flowers clinging to tiny pockets of nourishment.

The slate museum at Llanberis not long after opening—looking as if the men could be back at any moment.

You can even go underground. Would the old miners have found it strange to see people paying to look at where they toiled?

It takes a very long time for plants to become established in hard slatey rocks—when they do, they can be strikingly beautiful.

Mining and quarrying remains.

Nant Gwrtheyrn, as it was.

Signs at Barmouth. 'Open on Sundays During Season' harks back to the times of 'dry' Sundays; severe restrictions on serving alcoholic drinks and opening hours.

I could, I suppose, have included Milford's fish dock within the 'Seaside' section, but it seems to link much more closely to industry than holidays, so I fitted it in here. Now Milford remains a busy and successful fishing port—a crucial selling point being its westerly location, closer to the fishing grounds than most of its competitors - but things did not necessarily look so positive in the 1970s. I know this is an industry which runs to unconventional hours, so not seeing anyone about at a particular point may mean little. But initial appearances weren't good. A large, worn board advertised fish trains to Liverpool, Nottingham, Bournemouth and all sorts of other places. The trains hadn't actually run for many years, of course, and the board's only practical current use seemed to be to advertise a darts competition. The Fish Trades restaurant was closed, the wind-worn buildings around the dock were eye-catching but deserted.

The board suggests that fish trains leave for Liverpool, Nottingham and many other parts of Britain early in the morning. But unfortunately that hasn't been the case for a long time.

A tap is running, but not much else: in the 1970s, business isn't what it was, although 40 years later Milford is one of the biggest fish ports in Britain.

Not many signs of life at the Fish Trades restaurant.

Above The support industries' fortunes were tightly linked to the fortunes of the port. In the 1970s, demand for wire trawl warps and the future didn't look entirely bright.

Left A westerly gale can hit Milford hard: one way of keeping out the worst of it all, using slates as shingles.

Llangollen.

But finally, I can't apologise to my friends in North East Wales enough. I went there many times in the 1970s, and go still, I just haven't any interesting photographs. Here's just a token image of Llangollen—home of the International Eistedford and the Llangollen Railway.

ten

An End Piece

I have had to look through several thousand images to get this far, but it's been no hardship. The memories have been flooding back and it's been fascinating to reflect on what has changed and what has not. The 1970s were well before devolution, of course. The 1989 referendum vote went in favour by a very narrow majority only, but the Assembly now seems to have been there for ages, with questions about its role and purpose arising infrequently at most. The Welsh language seems stronger, with more Welsh medium education and institutions like S4C. And on average we are better off, despite the last few years.

It's true to say that in the older industrial areas people continue to die earlier than people do in the suburbs, but that's not unknown in many parts of the United Kingdom.

Education has traditionally been a source of pride throughout Wales: that has changed to some extent with worrying evidence of poorer literacy and numeracy in schools, and some skill shortages for employers to face. Again, though, Wales it not the only place where you can hear these sorts of comments.

Indeed, wider trends have been behind all sorts of fundamental changes in Wales, rather than decisions made in Wales, or changes in Welsh policies or social attitudes.

Employers have supply chains which span regional, national and frequently continental boundaries, for example. In 1970, throughout the world 'computing' meant vast, temperamental main frames, cosseted by their teams are of minders and worshippers. Tablets, smartphones and the rest were beyond comprehension. This is a digression, but the first personal computer I got my hands on (in the early 1980s) was an Osborne. It weighed a great deal and was essentially useless for what I needed it to do. I spilled a cup of tea over its keyboard which may not have improved our relationship, but all in all I wasn't sorry to see it go, not one little bit.

For a while during the 1970s and afterwards, new jobs arrived in factories manu-facturing TVs, microwaves and all manner of other consumer goods—often owned by Japanese firms, but with Germans, Americans, Koreans and various others... not forgetting some from other parts of the UK. Most of them moved on again, but they seem to have provided skills and an element of self-confidence about manufacturing more generally. And, with major retail redevelopment followed by a rash of flats and office developments Cardiff started to look like a sophisticated modern city and signs of investment life became apparent in another towns and city centres too.

But quite a bit hasn't changed as much as a lot of people expected. Some continuity is a very good thing: Wales remains, above all, a great place to live and work. Yet that isn't quite the whole story. Transport investment has been patchy: driving from South Wales to North Wales along the A470 still takes a very long time; the design of the diesels going to London and up the valleys now date back 30 years or more.

Maybe it's the continuing problem of getting sufficient good quality jobs into the former coal mining areas which is most worrying. After all, it's three quarters of a century since the former Prince of Wales declared 'Something must be done' in Dowlais. The Special Areas (Development and Improvement) Act dates from 1934. But these are bigger issues than I can address, particularly in a book of nostalgic photographs.

Looking forwards prompts a lot more questions: social, technical, economic—you name it. And what should I do about a lot more photographs in a drawer next to me as I write this? We'll just have to see.

Cardiff: starting to look like a world-class city.

The north end of Cardiff's docks: not much sign of the burning buses.

Opposite above With a barrage, permanent high water conceals a lot of things, for good or ill. You won't be seeing sticky brown mud, or abandon steamers any time soon.

Opposite below Ebbw Vale has moved in a different direction. The Christ Church spire is still there, holding out confidently against the world around it: there's been a Garden Festival and some new housing. No hint now of rolling mills or coke works as a dramatic backdrop (or provider of highly-paid jobs).

Unfortunately things haven't gone so well in Zion.